Sixty
Shades
of Bonking

A I Plenderleith

RAVETTE PUBLISHING

©2013 by Allan Plenderleith
www.allanplenderleith.com

All rights reserved

This edition published in Great Britain by
Ravette Publishing Limited 2013
PO Box 876, Horsham, West Sussex RH12 9GH

ISBN: 978-1-84161-369-7

Jeff was having trouble finishing off his romantic poem.

Hungry for love, Maude tries computer dating.

To perk things up, the office introduced Casual Sex Fridays.

After dinner, Maude turned on
the dishwasher.

To show Maude he loved her,
Jeff bought her a dozen roses.

Maude discovers why
Flagpole Pete was so-called.

The way to a woman's heart: flowers.
The way to a woman's bed: vodka!

Debbie likes a bit of fourplay.

A Guide to CALORIE LOSS during SEX!

	CALORIES
REMOVING CLOTHES:	18
TRYING TO UNHOOK BRA:	300
LIFTING HER UP THE STAIRS:	746
PUTTING ON CONDOM:	24
TRYING TO FIND CONDOM: AFTER IT PINGS OFF:	98
MISSIONARY POSITION:	36
HER ON TOP:	76
LEGS UP, HEAD BACK, HANGING FROM THE CEILINGLIGHT WITH A TRIPLE BACKWARDS SOMERSAULT:	2947
EARTH-MOVING ORGASM:	51
ATTEMPT TO WAKE UP MAN FOR ANOTHER GO:	18
SEARCH FOR MISSING KNICKERS:	95

Maude couldn't do any more work
that day as her inbox was full.

Every morning, Jeff gives Maude the old one gun salute.

Dug had heard
Felicity likes a good hard banging.

As the instructions said,
before laying the patio slabs
Jeff put down some hard core.

The new box of chocolates especially designed to satisfy women.

During sex, Jeff tried to hold back for as long as possible, but finally he could hold on no more.

Norah would attract men with her massive pair of honkers.

At the weekend,
Jeff got Maude in the sack.

Dug had not in fact asked Patsy to show him her "shaven raven"

Patsy's date had promised to serve her posh food in his apartment then liquor out on the balcony.

Maude attempts to turn on
her man by not wearing underwear.

Things NOT to say during sex!

Jeff goes paintballing.

Maude sexes up her big pants with some kinky peekaboo holes.

When Jeff walked in to the bedroom,
Maude was already playing with herself.

Patsy poses nude for a magazine.

Jeff asks to try some
"same sex" action.

Never burp during a kiss.

Dug meets a girl who is a
real sex kitten.

Patsy turns on Dave by
shaking her booty.

Patsy was rushed to casualty with something stuck in her throat.

Maude asked Jeff to go and
strain the spuds.

Dug hates getting a sweater on his birthday.

To get Samantha into bed,
Dug sweet talks her.

Dave asked his girlfriend
for a threesome.

This wasn't the blu-ray disc Jeff thought he had ordered.

Once again, Jeff's mind had drifted off onto other things whilst doing the gardening.

Older ladies – always wear a bra
on windy days.

Patsy's man was the only good looking bloke at the disco – everyone else was "butters".

Chat up lines women <u>WANT</u> to hear!

I earn over £40k!

I own a chocolate factory!

I own a discount designer shoe chain!

Aren't shoe shops FAB!

I HATE football!

On romantic nights, Jeff makes that extra special effort.

Dug asked Debbie if he could see her chuff.

When they got home, Dave said he
was going to rip Debbie's knickers off.

Patsy had just been
poked on Facebook.

Unfortunately, Maude had
a fear of worms.

Dug couldn't wait to get home
to see Barbara's "giant pussy."

Maude likes doggy fashion.

Later in life,
Lily would regret
getting implants.

Dug loves a girl with enormous jugs.

Patsy's man was a real good looker.

Patsy was impressed by the size of her new boyfriend's manhood.

Jeff didn't have the heart to tell
Lily it was just a mushroom.

Dug's new pants were a hit
with the ladies.

The doctor didn't need to ask how Jeff had sprained his tongue.

Jeff had asked Maude to wear
something see-through.

Maude found Jeff much sexier
when he wore his contacts.

As Jeff's attractive golf partner
bent over to tee up, Jeff whacked
one out in the rough.

These weren't the beef curtains
Jeff was hoping to see.

Patsy had promised Dave
a wet t-shirt show.

Maude had a great rack.

Patsy's new man was a grate kisser.

To get them in the mood for love
Jeff puts on a blue movie.

Unfortunately, Maude's hopes
were quickly dashed.

Valentine card sizes and what they mean.

Maude was thrilled Jeff gave her a relaxing back massage, even though the football was on.

Unfortunately due to the credit crunch, chocolate willies weren't what they used to be.

Just for a change,
Jeff wanted to come through
the back door.

Other ODD SQUAD books available …

	ISBN	PRICE
Hardback Gift Books (127 x 127 mm)		
Cartoons to Cheer up a Grumpy Old Git	978-1-84161-360-4	£4.99
Cartoons to Cheer up a Stroppy Mare	978-1-84161-361-1	£4.99
I Love Beer	978-1-84161-238-6	£5.99
I Love Dad	978-1-84161-252-2	£5.99
I Love Mum	978-1-84161-249-2	£5.99
I Love Poo	978-1-84161-240-9	£5.99
I Love Sex	978-1-84161-241-6	£4.99
I Love Wine	978-1-84161-239-3	£4.99
I Love Xmas	978-1-84161-262-1	£4.99
Paperback Books (210 x 148 mm)		
The Odd Squad's Book for Blokes	978-1-84161-319-2	£5.99
The Odd Squad's Guide to Love	978-1-84161-324-6	£5.99
The Odd Squad's Hot Cross Puns	978-1-84161-323-9	£5.99
The Odd Squad's Guide to Poo	978-1-84161-325-3	£6.99

HOW TO ORDER:

Please send a cheque/postal order in £ sterling, made payable to 'Ravette Publishing'
for the cover price of the book/s and allow the following for post & packing …

UK & BFPO	70p for the first book & 40p per book thereafter
Europe & Eire	£1.30 for the first book & 70p per book thereafter
Rest of the world	£2.20 for the first book & £1.10 per book thereafter

RAVETTE PUBLISHING LTD
PO Box 876, Horsham, West Sussex   RH12 9GH
Tel: 01403 711443   Fax: 01403 711554   Email: ingrid@ravettepub.co.uk

Prices and availability are subject to change without prior notice.